Piano / Vocal / Guitar

Great American Songwriters

59 Songs by 27 Composers & Lyricists

ISBN 0-7935-8948-7

HAL•LEONARD®
CORPORATION

7777 W. BLUEMOUND RD. P.O. BOX 13819 MILWAUKEE, WI 53213

Visit Hal Leonard Online at
www.halleonard.com

S0-BKT-037

Great American Songwriters

Alphabetical by Song Title

Great American Songwriters

Alphabetical by Featured Composers & Lyricists

Great American Songwriters

Featured Songwriters

HAROLD ARLEN
1905-1986

Featured songs in this collection: "Come Rain or Come Shine," "Stormy Weather," "Last Night When We Were Young"

Born Hyman Arluck, Harold Arlen's earliest aspiration was to become a singer. His father was a cantor in a Buffalo synagogue, and his mother played the piano. When those dreams never materialized, Arlen took to the piano. His first hit came in 1928 with "Get Happy" (lyrics by Ted Koehler). Ironically, it was songwriter Harry Warren who introduced Arlen to Koehler. After writing three Broadway musicals, *Earl Carroll Vanities, You Said It and Life Begins at 8:40,* Arlen moved to Hollywood where he concentrated on film scores for most of the 1930s. For the next 30 years, working with various lyricists such as E.Y. Harburg, Johnny Mercer and Ira Gershwin, Arlen composed such standards as the 1939 Oscar-winner "Over the Rainbow," "It's Only a Paper Moon," "Blues in the Night," "That Old Black Magic," "Stormy Weather," "Ac-cent-tchu-ate the Positive" and "The Man That Got Away," which became a later-day Judy Garland showstopper. In the 1950 MGM film *Summerstock,* Warren's score for the movie was supplemented (much to his frustration) by "Get Happy," which proved to be yet another unforgettable number for Judy Garland. Arlen returned to Broadway periodically in the 1940s and '50s. His two most successful shows, both written in collaboration with Harburg, were *Bloomer Girl* (a Civil War musical) and *Jamaica,* which was set in the Caribbean and starred Lena Horne. Perhaps the greatest compliment ever paid to Arlen came from arguably the finest composer of the popular musical era, George Gershwin. He called Arlen, "the most original of us all." Garland wasn't the only singer who especially loved Arlen's songs. Early in her career, Barbra Streisand sang a good deal of Arlen, including guesting on an album Arlen recorded.

IRVING BERLIN
1888-1989

Featured songs in this collection: "Blue Skies," "Cheek to Cheek," "What'll I Do?"

Perhaps Jerome Kern summed up best Irving Berlin's almost mythic status as a composer/lyricist of popular American songs. "Irving Berlin has no place in American music," Kern said. "He is American music." Certainly no other popular composer has ever approached Berlin's long track record of hit songs, a streak that began in 1906 with his first published song, "Marie from Sunny Italy," and continued well into the 1950s. Born Israel Baline, Berlin, along with his family, emigrated to America in 1892, after a Cossack pogrom drove them out of their village of Temun, Russia. Growing up poor on New York City's Lower East Side, young Berlin earned money singing in Bowery saloons, and eventually became a song plugger. After his first success with "Marie," Berlin threw himself into his new-found vocation with single-minded determination. In 1911, he wrote "Alexander's Ragtime Band," which became an international sensation and sold over one million copies of sheet music. Berlin followed up that success with other hit ragtime songs, and, in 1914, composed the score for his first Broadway musical, *Watch Your Step.* Berlin entered the army in 1918 and wrote the music for *Yip, Yip,*

Yaphank, which included "Oh! How I Hate to Get Up in the Morning" and "Mandy." Back in civilian life, Berlin's string of hits continued with scores for *The Ziegfeld Follies of 1919*, which included "A Pretty Girl is Like a Melody," and his own Music Box Revues. He also continued to write individual song hits like "Always" and "Remember." During the 1930s and '40s, Berlin shuttled between Hollywood and Broadway, contributing scores to a number of Fred Astaire/Ginger Rogers films at RKO, with such songs as, "Top Hat," "Cheek to Cheek," "Change Partners" and "Let's Face the Music and Dance." Kate Smith introduced Berlin's "God Bless America" in 1938 and another national anthem was born. In 1942, Berlin won an Academy Award for "White Christmas," from the movie *Holiday Inn* starring Bing Crosby and Astaire. Crosby's recording of the tune holds the distinction of selling more records than any other song in history. During World War II, Berlin was again called on to write a service musical. He responded with *This Is the Army*. A song from that show, "This Is the Army, Mr. Jones" became a hit with servicemen returning home from the war. After the war, Berlin contributed the scores to several Broadway musicals, including his greatest theater triumph, *Annie Get Your Gun*, written for the star of the show, Ethel Merman playing Annie Oakley. Subsequent Broadway scores include *Call Me Madam*, *Mr. President*, and *Miss Liberty*. In true Berlin tradition, each show gave birth to songs that have become standards. Berlin basically retired from public life in the early 1960s, but lived on another 25 years to past the age of 100!

SAMMY CAHN
1914-1993

**Featured songs in this collection: "Call Me Irresponsible,"
"Three Coins in the Fountain"**

It wasn't a Steinway and it didn't even have white and black keys. In fact, the composing instrument of choice for four-time Oscar-winning lyricist Sammy Cahn wasn't even a piano. He used an IBM manual typewriter to create the words to such American song standards as "High Hopes," "All the Way," "Three Coins in the Fountain," "I've Heard That Song Before," "Let It Snow," "Call Me Irresponsible," "Come Fly with Me," "(Chicago Is) My Kind of Town," "Love and Marriage" and dozens of others, mostly in collaboration with Jule Styne and James Van Heusen. As Cahn explained in a 1981 interview in his Beverly Hills home, he began his musical education by writing parodies of popular songs while attending high school in his native New York City. "The greatest exercise for a beginning songwriter is to write parodies," he said. "Education is a tool, especially for a man who deals in words." Cahn called his ability to write lyrics an unexplainable miracle. "I put the paper in and type. That's it. No margin for error, no paper strewn around the floor. It never fails. It's a miracle and I'm pleased to be part of the miracle. I say this most modestly," he added. "I'm not calling myself a miracle worker. The point is, I just sit and type, and there's no way in the world it doesn't come out. I don't write the songs as much as the song writes me." Inspiration for a new song lyric was never more than a phone call away. "People always ask me, which comes first, the words or the music? It's the phone call. If the phone stops ringing, I will stop writing." For Cahn, the phone never stopped ringing.

Great American
Songwriters

HOAGY CARMICHAEL
1899-1981

Featured songs in this collection: "Georgia on My Mind," "Star Dust"

Hoagy Carmichael, more than any other golden age songwriter, contributed to his own legend by appearing in supporting roles in movies. The composer of such perennials as "Star Dust," "Georgia on My Mind" and "In the Cool, Cool, Cool of the Evening" rode a mule, wore a stovepipe hat, and sang his hit "Ole Buttermilk Sky" in *Canyon Passage*. He taught double amputee Harold Russell how to play "Chopsticks" with his hooks in *The Best Years of Our Lives*, and he was the waterfront piano man in *To Have and Have Not*, starring Humphrey Bogart and Lauren Bacall. In 1980, retired from the screen and composing, Carmichael was living in a condominium in La Costa, California, and had this to say in an interview: "I never had any formal musical schooling. When I was a boy I worked in a 5-and-10-cent store set in the shadow of Indiana University. My mother played ragtime, and when I was about 12 years old she showed me some basic chord structures." Carmichael developed his piano technique at the Kappa Sigma fraternity dances while attending Indiana University. "Hot music" was a pleasant diversion, but certainly not substantial enough to build a career on. So, to please his father, Carmichael graduated with a law degree. Carmichael's recording career yielded a catalogue of 125-130 published songs, a figure he described as "way low." However, what he lacked in quantity, he made up in quality numbering several jazz and blues standards among his hits. In the 25 years that he wrote songs and themes for films, Carmichael won an Oscar in 1950 for "In the Cool, Cool, Cool of the Evening."

WALTER DONALDSON & GUS KAHN
1893-1947 & 1886-1941

Featured songs in this collection: "Love Me or Leave Me," "My Buddy"

Whether working as a team or writing with other collaborators, composer Walter Donaldson and lyricist Gus Kahn wrote dozens of hit songs during their all-too-brief lives. Donaldson was born in Brooklyn, New York and under his mother's tutelage (she was a pianist and music teacher) showed an early affinity toward music. By the time he was in high school, he had begun to compose. By 1915, he had written his first hits, "Back Home in Tennessee," "You'd Never Know That Old Home Town of Mine" and "We'll Have a Jubilee in My Old Kentucky Home." In 1918, he wrote, "The Daughter of Rosie O'Grady." As an employee of the Irving Berlin music publishing company in the early 1920s, he wrote, "How Ya Gonna Keep 'Em Down on the Farm?" and the Al Jolson warhorse, "My Mammy." Gus Kahn was born in Coblenz, Germany. He and his family settled in Chicago when he was five. Turn-of-the-century Chicago was a hub for popular music, and Kahn became infatuated with this new and different sound. He began writing lyrics while still in school. He published his first song "I Wish I Had a Girl" in 1907. Just before World War I, he teamed with composer Egbert Van Alstyne for several hits, including "Sunshine and Roses," "Memories," "Pretty Baby" and "Sailing Away on the Henry Clay." In 1922, Donaldson met Kahn, who had recently relocated from Chicago to New York. They kicked-off their partnership with two back-to-back hits, "My Buddy" and "Carolina in the Morning." The two worked together off and on for nearly twenty years. A few of their other standards included "Yes, Sir, That's My Baby" and "That Certain Party." In 1928, Donaldson and Kahn wrote the score for the Eddie Cantor Broadway show *Whoopee!*, featuring the songs, "Makin' Whoopee!," "My Baby Just Cares for Me" and the Ruth Etting torch song, "Love Me or Leave Me." In the mid 1930s, they wrote the score for such films as *The Prize Fighter* and *The Lady and Kid Millions*, another Eddie Cantor vehicle. In collaboration with such composers as Isham Jones, Kahn also wrote the lyrics to "It Had to Be You" and "The One I Love Belongs to Somebody Else."

DUKE ELLINGTON
1899-1974

Featured songs in this collection: "It Don't Mean a Thing (If It Ain't Got That Swing)," "Satin Doll," "Sophisticated Lady"

He was born Edward Kennedy Ellington in Washington, D.C. Just prior to starting high school, an upwardly mobile friend named Edgar McEntree insisted that any friend of his had to have a title of nobility. So he bestowed on Ellington the name Duke. It would prove a worthy moniker. Ellington took up piano at an early age and wrote his first song at age 15. After graduating from high school in 1917, he gave up a scholarship to study commercial art at Pratt Institute in Brooklyn, and instead pursued a career in music. He formed a jazz band in Washington and moved it to New York City in 1923. The group's first regular gig at the Hollywood Club (later renamed the Kentucky Club) lasted four years. Ellington first attracted national attention when he and his band opened at New York City's famed Cotton Club on Dec. 4, 1927. The gig lasted until 1932 and gave Ellington a home base from which to experiment and grow as a musician, bandleader, composer, conductor and arranger. While at the Cotton Club, Ellington wrote such standards as "Mood Indigo," "Creole Rhapsody" and "Sophisticated Lady." During the 1930s, Ellington and his band toured the United States and Europe. Compositions during this period included "Solitude," "Prelude to a Kiss," "Do Nothin Till You Hear from Me" and "I'm Beginning to See the Light." Billy Strayhorn, Ellington's longtime arranger and collaborator, played a pivotal role in creating the "Ellington Sound." Ellington's work across the spectrum of jazz, popular and concert music has made it difficult to lump him into a narrowly defined musical category. Ellington's legacy also includes larger orchestral works, such as "New World A-Comin," "Echoes of Harlem," "Harlem Suite" and "Such Sweet Thunder."

SAMMY FAIN
1902-

Featured songs in this collection: "I'll Be Seeing You," "You Brought a New Kind of Love to Me"

A hitmaker for some 50 years, the name Sammy Fain doesn't register the same recognition as many of his songwriting contemporaries, men like Gershwin, Porter and Berlin. In some cases, his work is often confused with that of another Sammy, Sammy Cahn. It doesn't seem to matter that he wrote two Academy Award-winning songs, "Secret Love" and "Love Is a Many Splendored Thing" and dozens of other hits for stage and screen. Born in New York City, Fain attended public school in New York State's Sullivan County, where his father was a cantor. Fain taught himself how to play the piano and began to compose at an early age. After high school, Fain moved to Manhattan to be closer to the music business. His first job in the field was as a stockroom boy for a music publisher. During breaks, he would sneak into the audition room and play his own compositions. When his boss caught him, instead of showing him the door, he promoted Fain to song plugger. In 1925, his first song, "Nobody Knows What a Red-Headed Mama Can Do" was published. That same year the struggling Fain met Irving Kahal, who became his lyricist until Kahal's death in 1942. Their output of hits included: "Let a Smile Be Your Umbrella," "Wedding Bells Are Breaking Up That Old Gang of Mine," "When I Take My Sugar to Tea," "You Brought a New Kind of Love to Me," "I Can Dream Can't I?" and "I'll Be Seeing You," which became a misty-eyed anthem of separation during World War II. After Kahal's death, Fain collaborated with several lyricists on material for motion pictures. His two Oscar winners and four other nominated tunes were written with Paul Francis Webster.

DOROTHY FIELDS
1905-1974

Featured songs in this collection: "Close as Pages in a Book," "I Can't Give You Anything but Love"

No one broke the songwriting gender barrier more than Dorothy Fields. The Fields name was synonymous with show business. Her father was vaudeville comedian Lew Fields, and her brothers included librettist-producer Herbert, and playwright-librettist Joseph. After abandoning a career as a high school art teacher, Fields teamed with composer Jimmy McHugh to write the lyrics for the revue *Blackbirds of 1928*. The show included the hits "Diga, Diga, Doo" and "I Can't Give You Anything but Love." They contributed to Broadway shows and movies for several years, producing a steady stream of hits, including "I Feel a Song Comin' On" and "I'm in the Mood for Love." Fields met composer Jerome Kern in 1935 when they, along with McHugh, wrote "Lovely to Look At." That started the Fields-Kern collaboration culminating in the 1936 Oscar-winning song "The Way You Look Tonight" for the Fred Astaire and Ginger Rogers RKO musical *Swingtime*. Other notable lyrics include "On the Sunny Side of the Street" and "Pick Yourself Up." In collaboration with her brother Herbert, Fields wrote screenplays and a series of hit Broadway musicals, including the librettos for three Cole Porter shows, *Let's Face It*, *Something for the Boys* and *Mexican Hayride*. The Fields were about to work with Kern again on a musical based on sharpshooter Annie Oakley. When Kern died, they instead teamed with Irving Berlin, writing the libretto for the classic *Annie Get Your Gun*. Fields also worked with composers Sigmund Romberg and Arthur Schwartz.

GEORGE GERSHWIN
1898-1937

Featured songs in this collection: "Aren't You Kind of Glad We Did?," "Somebody Loves Me," "Swanee"

George Gershwin left an astounding body of work in a prolific life tragically cut short at age 38 from a brain tumor. Scores of sophisticated hit songs, the Pulitzer Prize-winning musical *Of Thee I Sing*, the great American opera *Porgy and Bess* and three legendary orchestral works, "Rhapsody in Blue," "Concerto in F" and "An American in Paris" are part of the Gershwin musical legacy. Born in Brooklyn, New York, Gershwin showed an early affinity for athletic competition, not music. It was only when his mother bought a piano intended for his older brother, Ira, did Gershwin quickly start to show himself a musical prodigy. Alongside his interest in the cutting edge trends of popular music of the day, he studied piano and composition quite seriously in a traditional way with some remarkable private teachers, completely propelled by George's ferocious appetite for learning about music. He quit school at age 15 for a job as a pianist with Remick Music, and soon after, published his first song, "When You Want 'Em, You Can't Get 'Em." Success came quickly for the wunderkind composer. In 1919, he wrote the score for *La La Lucille*, and later that year entertainer Al Jolson made Gershwin's "Swanee" a worldwide hit. Gershwin was lead composer for the series of *George White Scandals* from 1920 to 1929. Out of one of those shows came the standard "Somebody Loves Me." Although Gershwin had teamed with brother Ira sporadically (their first song together was in 1918), the two collaborated almost exclusively beginning with "Lady, Be Good" in 1924 until Gershwin's death in 1937. The smash Broadway show included the trendsetting song "Fascinating Rhythm" and "Oh, Lady Be Good." The Gershwins' string of Broadway successes included *Oh Kay!*, *Funny Face*, *Rosalie*, *Strike Up the Band*, and *Girl Crazy*. These shows featured such songs as " 'S Wonderful," "Funny Face," "He Loves and She Loves," "How Long Has This Been Going On?," "I've Got Rhythm" and "I've Got a Crush on You." Gershwin first became interested in writing an opera in 1926, after reading DuBose Heyward's short novel *Porgy*, about the experience of poor blacks on Catfish Row in Charleston, South Carolina. Prior commitments prevented him from completing *Porgy and Bess* until 1935. The show opened to mixed reviews and a shorter run than hoped for, but it was eventually recognized as a masterpiece, and today is in the repertoire of the Metropolitan Opera. After

"Porgy," Gershwin returned to Hollywood where he wrote the scores to the Astaire-Rogers musical, *Shall We Dance*, featuring "They Can't Take That Away from Me" and "Let's Call the Whole Thing Off." The Astaire solo effort, *A Damsel in Distress*, included "Nice Work If You Can Get It" and "A Foggy Day (In London Town)." The last song Gershwin wrote, "Love Is Here to Stay" appeared in the 1938 film *The Goldwyn Follies*. His sudden death after a brief struggle with a brain tumor threw the whole country into grief. Gershwin's music continues to appear in film scores and his orchestral works are still played by symphonies throughout the world to enraptured audiences. More than any other of the songwriters of the golden age, he defined the American music of the twentieth century.

IRA GERSHWIN
1896-1983

**Featured songs in this collection: "Aren't You Kind of Glad We Did?,"
"I Can't Get Started With You""The Man That Got Away,"**

One of the greatest lyricists in American musical theater, perennially shy and retiring Ira Gershwin, shunned the spotlight that was mostly cast on his younger brother and long-time collaborator, George. The first piano in the Gershwin home was bought for Ira, but it was soon determined that George had greater musical talent, and the lessons went to him. Ira Gershwin attended New York's Townsend Harris Hall and City College. Since boyhood Ira was obsessed with light verse, and kept scrapbooks of his favorites. He also studied the Gilbert & Sullivan operettas in great detail. He earned his first dollar as a wordsmith in 1917 for a humorous paragraph that he sold to the magazine *Smart Set*. In 1918, Ira and George teamed for the first time on "The Real American Folk Song," which was introduced by Nora Bayes in the show *Ladies First*. After collaborating with Vincent Youmans on the Broadway show *Two Little Girls in Blue* in 1921, Ira worked again with his brother on a failed musical called *A Dangerous Maid*. Their first hit collaboration was the 1924 show *Lady Be Good*, which starred Fred and Adele Astaire and included such standards as the title tune, "Fascinating Rhythm" and "The Half of It, Dearie Blues." For the show *Tip Toes*, Ira contributed "That Certain Feeling" and "Sweet and Low-Down." Other show songs written with his brother during the 1920s amount to a treasure trove of classic standards. They include "Do, Do, Do," "Someone to Watch Over Me," "He Loves and She Loves," "'S Wonderful" and "I've Got a Crush on You." In 1931, Ira wrote the lyrics to the political satire musical *Of Thee I Sing*, and for his contribution was awarded the Pulitzer Prize. He contributed song lyrics to the 1935 opera *Porgy and Bess*. After the opera, there was one last wonderful period of songs for the Gershwin brothers, working together in Hollywood, writing primarily for Fred Astaire. The brothers wrote the score for *Shall We Dance?*, *A Damsel in Distress*, and were working on the score for *The Goldwyn Follies* when George suddenly died. These California songs of late 1936 and the first months of 1937 include some of their best: "A Foggy Day," "Love Is Here to Stay," "Let's Call the Whole Thing Off," "Nice Work If You Can Get It," "They Can't Take That Away from Me." After George's death in 1937, Gershwin worked with many of the best composers on Broadway and in Hollywood. In 1941, he collaborated with Kurt Weill on *Lady in the Dark*. In 1944, he worked with Jerome Kern on the movie *Cover Girl*, which starred Gene Kelly and Rita Hayworth. One of their songs, "Long Ago (And Far Away)," became an instant hit and Academy Award nominee for Best Song. Perhaps Gershwin's most memorable tune after the death of his brother was written to a Harold Arlen melody. The song, "The Man That Got Away," was introduced by Judy Garland in *A Star Is Born*.

OSCAR HAMMERSTEIN II
1895-1960

Featured songs in this collection: "The Folks Who Live On the Hill," "It Might as Well Be Spring," "Some Enchanted Evening"

Oscar Hammerstein II played a significant role in revolutionizing the American musical theater by writing the book and lyrics for the two most influential musicals in Broadway history: *Show Boat* and *Oklahoma!*. Born in New York City, it seemed Hammerstein was destined for a career in the theater. His grandfather and namesake, Oscar (I), was a producer and impresario in grand opera and built the Manhattan Opera House. His father, William, managed a vaudeville theater. And his uncle, Arthur, was a Broadway producer. While attending Columbia University, he wrote and appeared in several varsity show productions. He even appeared in one show with classmate Lorenz Hart. He worked his way up the theatrical ladder first as a stage hand, then a playwright. In 1920, he teamed with Otto Harbach and Herbert Stothart on the moderately successful show *Tickle Me*. In 1924, Harbach and Hammerstein provided Rudolf Friml with book and lyrics for *Rose Marie*. In addition to the title song, the show produced the hit, "Indian Love Call." Later that year, Harbach and Hammerstein teamed with Jerome Kern on the Marilyn Miller vehicle *Sunny*. Out of the collaboration came the Hammerstein-Kern interest in Edna Ferber's novel about riverboat life on the Mississippi. Before *Show Boat* hit the boards in 1927, Hammerstein squeezed in another show with Sigmund Romberg, *The Desert Song*. *Show Boat*, with the exception of the song "Bill," featured lyrics and book by Hammerstein. During the 1930s, Hammerstein continued to collaborate with a number of composers, most often with Kern, but also with Romberg and Friml. It was during a dry spell for Hammerstein in the early 1940s that he decided to collaborate with longtime friend Richard Rodgers on *Oklahoma!* after his partnership with Lorenz Hart had largely deteriorated, shortly before Hart's death. After *Oklahoma!* theatergoers could expect a new Rodgers and Hammerstein show every couple of years during the 1940s and 1950s. The collaboration was so beloved and revered that it practically became an American institution. Their subsequent classic shows included *Carousel* (1945), *State Fair* (1945, film), *Allegro* (1947), *South Pacific* (1949), *The King and I* (1951), *Me and Juliet* (1953), *Pipe Dream* (1955), *Cinderella* (1957, for television), *Flower Drum Song* (1958) and *The Sound of Music* (1959). An infrequent visitor to Hollywood, Hammerstein did pick up two Best Song Oscars for his lyrics to "The Last Time I Saw Paris" and "It Might as Well Be Spring."

LORENZ HART
1895-1943

Featured songs in this collection: "Bewitched," "Glad to Be Unhappy," "You Took Advantage of Me"

Known as the little man with the big talent, Lorenz (Larry, to his friends) was one of the most gifted lyricists of the golden era of popular song. Hart attended private schools, including Columbia University, where he attended the School of Journalism and performed and wrote material for college musical revues. In 1917, he left school before earning a degree, and the next year, a mutual friend Philip Leavitt, introduced Hart to a high school student with composing aspirations, Richard Rodgers. For the new songwriting team of Rodgers and Hart, success did not come quickly. In fact, in 1925, on the verge of quitting, they were invited to write the score for an amateur revue to benefit the Theatre Guild called *Garrick Gaieties*. The show was only scheduled for two performances, but made such an impression that a commercial run followed. The score included the breezy, catchy, sophisticated song "Manhattan," and it was the success of this song that really launched Rodgers and Hart. The team never considered disbanding the partnership again. For the remainder of the decade, Rodgers and Hart were the "Kings of Broadway," writing such songs as "The Blue Room," "Mountain Greenery," "My Heart Stood Still," "Thou Swell" and "With a Song in My Heart." They also had several shows in London. By 1930 America was in the Great Depression, and financially the best place for a songwriter to be was in Hollywood, so Rodgers and Hart headed west. They wrote some lovely songs there, "Blue Moon" (Hart actually was trying to write the most cliched lyric possible, and it turned out to be a hit) and "Isn't It Romantic?" particularly. Their biggest artistic success in film was *Love Me Tonight*, in which cinematography, dialogue and song were integrated to tell the story. But they were never comfortable in Tinseltown. They hated being treated as for-hire employees, rather than being at the creative center of a conception. Rodgers and Hart returned to New York in 1934, and elevated the musical theater to new heights with such shows as *Jumbo, On Your Toes, Babes in Arms, The Boys from Syracuse* and *Pal Joey.* A sampling of the hits from these shows include: "Where or When," "My Funny Valentine," "There's a Small Hotel," "This Can't Be Love," "I Could Write a Book" and "Bewitched." By 1942 Hart, plagued by severe addiction to alcohol and life-long self-destruction, became unable to continue working. He turned down Rodgers' proposal to make a musical of *Green Grow the Lilacs* (it later became *Oklahoma!*). Rodgers tried to help Hart, who was desperately depressed and self-destructive by this time, by initiating a revival of their 1927 show *A Connecticut Yankee* on Broadway. Hart wrote some of his wittiest lyrics for the added new songs (notably "To Keep My Love Alive"), but it was too late. He went on another drinking binge and died at age 48.

JEROME KERN
1885-1945

Featured songs in this collection: "Long Ago (And Far Away)," "The Song Is You," "The Way You Look Tonight"

Jerome Kern changed the American popular musical landscape permanently with his 1927 landmark show *Show Boat*. Noted music expert Cecil Smith in his book *Musical Comedy in America* wrote: "No other American piece of its vintage left so large a permanent musical legacy, and certainly no other surpassed it in quality." But there's much more to Kern's legacy than *Show Boat*. The composer, born in New York City, wrote dozens of scores for theater and film, including such songs as "Smoke Gets in Your Eyes," "They Didn't Believe Me," "All the Things You Are" and two Oscar-winners, "The Way You Look Tonight" and "The Last Time I Saw Paris." Kern's father held the water-sprinkling contract for Manhattan; his mother gave him his first piano lessons at an early age. Although his father wanted Kern to take over his water business, he opted to pursue a career in music. Kern studied at the New York College of Music then went to Europe to further his musical education. In 1904, just back from Europe, Kern started working as a song plugger, salesman and rehearsal pianist in Tin Pan Alley. The next year he wrote his first song hit, "How'd You Like to Spoon with Me?" Kern worked steadily, mostly interpolating songs for British shows playing on Broadway (British shows were the fashion). In 1915, he provided the music to an original American production *Very Good, Eddie,* as part of a producer's attempt to mount small-scale original musicals in the small Princess Theatre. It was a major hit and integrated music, lyrics and story. It was also decidedly American. With collaborators Guy Bolton and P.G. Wodehouse, Kern wrote the music for a series of popular shows, referred to by historians as the "Princess musicals," including *Oh Boy!, Leave It to Jane* and *Oh, Lady! Lady!* These shows inspired the young songwriting talents just about to emerge, who idolized Kern as their role model, talents such as George and Ira Gershwin, Richard Rodgers, Lorenz Hart and Cole Porter. With the exception of 1928, every year of the 1920s featured at least one new Kern show on Broadway. He teamed with Oscar Hammerstein II to buy the rights to Edna Ferber's novel of life on the Mississippi, *Show Boat*. The show produced the standards "Ol' Man River," "Make Believe," "Why Do I Love You?" and "Bill." It also was a serious attempt to break from the operetta format of the day, and to build serious stories and real characters in the form of an American musical. Other hit shows followed on Broadway, including *Sweet Adeline* and *Roberta*. From the mid 1930s until his death, Kern spent most of his career in Hollywood writing songs for the movies, including the Fred Astaire-Ginger Rogers movie musical *Swing Time* which he wrote with Dorothy Fields. His movie work was often with his longtime collaborator Oscar Hammerstein II. "Long Ago (And Far Away)," written with Ira Gershwin, won the Oscar as Best Song in 1944. In 1945, Kern returned to New York to begin work on a new musical based on the life of sharpshooter Annie Oakley to be called *Annie Get Your Gun*. Soon after he arrived, he died suddenly of complications from a heart attack.

BURTON LANE
1912-1997

**Featured songs in this collection: "How Are Things in Glocca Morra,"
"Too Late Now"**

Call it happenstance or maybe just perfect timing, but Burton Lane was certainly in the right place at the right time throughout his rich career as a songwriter of Hollywood and Broadway musicals. In 1933, he wrote a little ditty called "Heigh-Ho, the Gang's All Here," for an MGM film that introduced the world to a promising hoofer from Broadway, Fred Astaire. Thirty-five years later, Lane helped Astaire bring down the curtain on his legendary career when the dancer starred in the 1968 film adaptation of Lane's and lyricist E.Y. Harburg's landmark Broadway show *Finian's Rainbow*. In between, Burton Lane wrote the movie scores of the 1951 film *Royal Wedding*, and the 1965 show *On a Clear Day You Can See Forever;* the 1970 film version starred Barbra Streisand. Lane collaborated with several lyricists throughout his career, including Harold Adamson, Frank Loesser, Alan Jay Lerner and "Yip" Harburg. Born in New York City, Lane developed a friendship in his teenage years with George Gershwin, a man who would become his mentor. In a 1996 interview Lane said, "For my money, George Gershwin is still the greatest songwriter who ever lived. Before I met him and Ira, I didn't know there was a career in songwriting for me. I didn't know if I would fit in anyplace." Like Gershwin before him, Lane wrote songs for Remicks, a large music publisher of the day in New York City. Before lighting out to Hollywood, Lane also wrote the scores for several shows staged by the Shubert Brothers in New York City. Burton Lane wasn't the most famous of the great songwriters, but his songs certainly deserve fame.

ALAN JAY LERNER & FREDERICK LOEWE
1918-1986 & 1904-1988

Featured songs in this collection: "Gigi," "If Ever I Would Leave You"

Yes, Alan Jay Lerner and Frederick Loewe did have careers apart from each other, but those individual accomplishments were overshadowed by five legendary works written together (four for stage, one for film): *My Fair Lady, Brigadoon, Paint Your Wagon, Camelot* and *Gigi*. Alan Jay Lerner, born in New York City, was one of three sons of Joseph L. Lerner, founder of a successful chain of women's clothing shops. He studied at Juilliard School of Music and graduated from Harvard. Frederick "Fritz" Loewe, born in Vienna, Austria, was the son of Edmund Loewe, a popular operetta tenor. By the age of four he was playing the piano, and at nine composed the tunes for a music hall sketch in which his father toured Europe. At 15, he wrote "Katrina," a song that sold three million copies in Europe. When the two joined forces in 1942, neither had enjoyed sustained success. Loewe's show *Great Lady* had a brief run on Broadway in 1938, and Lerner had written radio scripts and some Harvard Hasty Pudding Club shows. The first Lerner and Loewe collaboration was a musical adaptation of Barry Connor's farce *The Patsy*, renamed *Life of the Party* for a Detroit stock company. Their first two Broadway shows, *What's Up?* and *The Day Before Spring* both received a lukewarm response. But the third time was a charm. On March 13, 1947 the misty Scottish Highland village known as *Brigadoon* appeared on Broadway. Between *Brigadoon* and *Paint Your Wagon* in 1951, Lerner wrote *Love Life* with music by Kurt Weill, the screenplay and lyrics for the MGM film *Royal Wedding,* and the story and screenplay for *An American in Paris*. Lerner and Loewe's next collaboration after *Paint Your Wagon* came in 1956 with the immortal *My Fair Lady*. The show ran for a record 2,717 performances. In 1958, Lerner and Loewe went to Hollywood to work on the musical adaptation of the French novel by Colette, *Gigi*. The film took home Best Picture honors at the Academy Awards. Despite its accolades and achievements, it was practically the last original musical made at MGM -- the studio shut down their musical division the same year. Their final collaboration came in 1960 with the Broadway musical *Camelot*. Loewe then retired, and Lerner, who always had a reputation for being rather "difficult," continued collaborating with other composers, including Burton Lane and Leonard Bernstein. About his longtime partner, Lerner wrote, "There will never be another Fritz . . . Writing will never again be as much fun. A collaboration as intense as ours inescapably had to be complex. But I loved him more than I understood or misunderstood him, and I know he loved me more than he understood or misunderstood me."

FRANK LOESSER
1910-1969

Featured songs in this collection: "Baby, It's Cold Outside," "I Wish I Didn't Love You So"

If Frank Loesser had done nothing more than write the score (which he did) to *Guys and Dolls,* he would have left an impressive musical legacy. Loesser's contributions to popular music are far-reaching: lyricist and composer for screen and stage, occasional librettist, producer and musical publisher responsible for introducing such names as Meredith Willson, Richard Adler and Jerry Ross to the musical stage. Born in New York City, Loesser attended public schools and City College in New York (he flunked out after a year). Loesser's father was a piano teacher, but loathed popular music, forcing his son to teach himself how to play this music "on the sly." He wrote his first composition, "The May Party" at the age of six. He published his first song, "In Love with a Memory of You" with composer William Schuman in 1931. His real success as a songwriter came when he began a 10-year tenure at Paramount Pictures in 1937. His film hits included: "Jingle, Jangle, Jingle," with Joseph Lilley; "Small Fry" and "Two Sleepy People," with Hoagy Carmichael. He contributed to the war effort by serving as an Army private and writing the hit, "Praise the Lord and Pass the Ammunition." After his discharge, Loesser concentrated on the Broadway stage, but in 1949, he won an Academy Award for "Baby, It's Cold Outside," from the MGM Esther Williams' film *Neptune's Daughter.* His first Broadway hit came in 1948 with *Where's Charley?*, featuring Ray Bolger and the song, "Once in Love with Amy." Two years later, Loesser outdid himself, with both words and music to *Guys and Dolls.* Loesser returned to Broadway four years later with the critically acclaimed *The Most Happy Fella.* His last Broadway triumph came in 1961 with *How to Succeed in Business Without Really Trying*, featuring the hit, "I Believe in You." In between his own shows, Loesser was responsible as producer for bringing to the stage such classics as *The Music Man, The Pajama Game* and *Damn Yankees.*

JOHNNY MERCER
1909-1976

Featured songs in this collection: "I'm Old Fashioned," "Moon River," "That Old Black Magic"

Johnny Mercer became our "Huckleberry Friend" with his haunting lyric to the Oscar-winning song "Moon River." The lyric was inspired from his childhood when he picked huckleberries in his native Savannah, Georgia. At 19, Mercer worked his way to New York on a steamship hoping to land a job on the Broadway stage. While attending an audition for the *Garrick Gaieties of 1929*, he heard that a song was needed for the show's star Sterling Holloway. In collaboration with another aspiring thespian, he wrote, "Out of Breath and Scared to Death of You." It became Mercer's first published song. Mercer collaborated with a number of composers through the years, most notably Harry Warren, Hoagy Carmichael, Harold Arlen and Henry Mancini. His three other Best Song Oscars came for his lyrics to "On the Atchison, Topeka and the Santa Fe," "In the Cool, Cool, Cool of the Evening" and "The Days of Wine and Roses." When he wasn't writing lyrics and appearing on radio broadcasts, Mercer found time to create Capitol Records and launch the careers of other successful songwriters and vocalists such as Nat "King" Cole and Peggy Lee. Though known primarily as a lyricist, Mercer composed the music to such standards as "Something's Gotta Give," "Dream," "I'm an Old Cowhand" and "I Wanna Be Around." If there's ever a doubt that Mercer is perhaps the most unheralded genius of the American popular song, consider his poetic words to these timeless tunes: "Blues in the Night," "Ac-cent-tchu-ate the Positive," "Laura," "Autumn Leaves," One for My Baby," "Come Rain or Come Shine" and "Summer Wind."

COLE PORTER

1893-1964

**Featured songs in this collection: "Ev'ry Time We Say Goodbye,"
"I've Got You Under My Skin," "Too Darn Hot"**

In many ways, Cole Porter's success as the composer of shimmering melodies and sophisticated verse seems improbable because he never had to pursue, out of necessity, a career in musical theater. Indeed, he never had to make a living at all. Born in Peru, Indiana, to wealth afforded by his grandfather's success in West Virginia coal and timber speculation, Porter was educated in the best schools. He began studying the violin at six and the piano at eight. By 1903, he had composed two songs, one of which, "The Bobolink Waltz," his mother had published. After graduating from Yale where he wrote two of the school's fight songs, "Bingo Eli Yale" and "Yale Bulldog Song," Porter entered Harvard's School of Music, against his grandfather's wishes. After his first Broadway show, *See America First*, flopped in 1916, Porter shipped off to North Africa and a stint with the French Foreign Legion. He made sure to pack his portable piano to entertain his comrades in arms. Sailing home shortly after the armistice that ended World War I, Porter met a producer on shipboard who commissioned him to write the score for the third "Hitchy-Koo" revue on Broadway (1919). One of Porter's songs, "An Old-Fashioned Garden," was a mild success. During most of the 1920s the Porters lived as European socialites in Paris and Venice, entertaining many guests. Porter continued to write songs for his own amusement, though his musical output was slight. In 1928, Porter's song "Let's Do It" scored a hit in the Broadway musical *Paris*. This song, with its naughty connotations and witty lyrics, is characteristic of much of Cole Porter's output. Almost every year after that, at least one, and sometimes two Porter musicals could be found running on the Broadway and London stages. His first major hit, *Fifty Million Frenchmen*, in 1929, included "You Do Something to Me" and "You Don't Know Paree." The same year, Porter wrote "What Is This Thing Called Love?" for the show *Wake Up and Dream*.

Porter's score to *Gay Divorce* (1932) included the classic "Night and Day" and "After You." Over the next few years he wrote the scores for *Anything Goes* (his best all-around show of the 1930s), Jubilee and *Red, Hot and Blue!* Then tragedy struck. In 1937, while out horseback riding, Porter suffered a crippling accident when the horse he was riding fell and crushed both his legs. Throughout the next two decades, Porter underwent dozens of painful operations to save them from being amputated. Despite this horrific setback and chronic pain, his composing work continued unabated. Besides writing the scores for a steady stream of stage shows, Porter wrote many movie songs that became classics, including "I've Got You Under My Skin," "You'd Be So Nice to Come Home To" and "Don't Fence Me In." In 1939, Porter had a hit with the score to *DuBarry Was a Lady,* and the next year wrote another smash, *Panama Hattie.* Even though these were successes, by the mid 1940s Cole Porter was a little out of fashion, and he had not had a hit song in several years. In 1948, Porter scored a great comeback and one of the greatest successes of his career with *Kiss Me, Kate.* The stage success was followed by a film version of the musical made by MGM. Porter had two other big hits in the 1950s on Broadway, *Can-Can* and *Silk Stockings.* After his score for the Gene Kelly musical *Les Girls* in 1957, Porter was in retirement. In fact, he was fairly reclusive for the rest of his years. In poor general health, Porter died after a kidney operation in a Santa Monica, California hospital. He was 71 years old.

Great American
Songwriters

RICHARD RODGERS
1902-1979

Featured songs in this collection: "Isn't It Romantic?," "Do I Love You Because You're Beautiful?," "My Funny Valentine"

First with Lorenz Hart and later with Oscar Hammerstein II, Richard Rodgers left a giant imprint in the history of the musical theater that is felt to this day. During his sixty-year career, Rodgers helped erase the last vestiges of European operetta from the American stage and was organically behind the emergence of the integrated book musical, most notably with his two landmark musicals *Pal Joey* (1940) and *Oklahoma!* (1943). Rodgers was raised in a musical household in Hammels Station, New York. His mother, a pianist, and his father, a doctor, would often vocalize around the house. Rodgers began piano lessons at age four and wrote his first song at 14. In 1919, while still in high school, he met Lorenz Hart, seven years his senior. Their collaboration lasted until Hart's death in 1943. They toiled together for several years before achieving their first hit song in 1926, "Manhattan." For both stage and movies, a sampling of their hit songs include: "The Blue Room," "Mountain Greenery," "My Heart Stood Still," "Thou Swell," "With a Song in My Heart," "Blue Moon," "Isn't It Romantic," "Where or When," "My Funny Valentine," "There's a Small Hotel," "This Can't be Love," "I Could Write a Book" and "Bewitched." Hart was self-destructive and struggled with alcoholism, and toward the end of his life work became difficult. Hart turned down working on what would be called *Oklahoma!*, and Rodgers turned to his old friend Oscar Hammerstein as a collaborator. Adjusting his style to accommodate his new lyricist, their first show was the monster hit, *Oklahoma!*. In 1945, Rodgers and Hammerstein wrote what Rodgers himself said was his favorite score, *Carousel.* That same year their original film musical *State Fair* was released. Rodgers and Hammerstein established themselves as the most successful theatrical collaboration since Gilbert and Sullivan. Not only did the men write successful musicals, they also were shrewd producers of their own shows and touring companies, as well as productions of other plays and musicals. In the late 1940s and 1950s they were the most powerful theatrical presence in New York. Their collaboration continued with *Allegro* (1947), *South Pacific* (1949), *The King and I* (1951), *Me and Juliet* (1953), *Pipe Dream* (1955), *Cinderella* (1957, for television), *Flower Drum Song* (1958) and *The Sound of Music* (1959). After Hammerstein's death, Rodgers wrote his own lyrics for the 1962 musical *No Strings*. He attempted a collaboration with Alan Jay Lerner, but the two men couldn't get along. Rodgers wrote the 1965 show *Do I Hear a Waltz?* with Stephen Sondheim. Those two didn't get along either. Rodgers pressed on with *Two by Two* (1970) with lyricist Martin Charnin, *Rex* (1976) with lyricist Sheldon Harnick, and *I Remember Mama* (1979) with Martin Charnin, which closed on Broadway just a few months before his death on December 30, 1979.

Arthur Schwartz & Howard Dietz
1900-1984 & 1896-1983

Featured songs in this collection: "By Myself," "That's Entertainment"

The songwriting team of composer Arthur Schwartz and lyricist Howard Dietz is best represented by their 1931 Broadway hit *The Band Wagon* featuring Adele and Fred Astaire, and the 1954 film version, again starring Astaire. Arthur Schwartz was born in Brooklyn, New York. He earned a master-of-arts degree from Columbia University in 1921 and a doctor of law from the same school in 1924. With little formal musical education, Schwartz began writing songs and placing them in such shows as *Dear Sir* and *The Grand Street Follies.* In 1928, Schwartz gave up on law all together and devoted his full-time energies to music. The catalyst for his career change was his friend, Howard Dietz. Dietz was born in New York City and during his career did everything from writing advertising copy to lyrics to children's books. During the heyday of the Hollywood studio system, Dietz ran MGM's powerful publicity department and even devised the company symbol Leo the Lion, and its corporate slogan: "Ars Gratia Artis." In 1929, the new team scored a hit on Broadway with the first *Little Show.* The musical launched the careers of comic Fred Allen and singer Libby Holman. It featured the tune, "I Guess I'll Have to Change My Plan," sung by Clifton Webb. The next two "Little Shows" failed to generate much excitement. *The Band Wagon* included such songs as "Dancing in the Dark" and "I Love Louisa." The

1953 film version also contained the show business anthem newly written for the movie, "That's Entertainment" and the lilting "By Myself," from their failed 1937 stage musical *Between the Devil*. In 1934, the team wrote the score for *Revenge with Music*. The show had a short run but produced the standards, "You and the Night and the Music" and "If There is Someone Lovelier than You." In the years following, Schwartz and Dietz went their separate ways. Schwartz continued to write for Broadway and Hollywood and also became a film producer. Dietz concentrated on his work for MGM. In 1948, the two briefly reteamed to provide the score for *Inside U.S.A.* starring Beatrice Lilly and Jack Haley. In the 1960s, the two collaborated again for the theatre on *The Gay Life* and *Jenny* (one of the most conspicuous flops in Broadway history).

JULE STYNE
1905-1994

Featured songs in this collection: "Just in Time," "People," "Small World"

There was never any doubt that Jule Styne was destined for a long and successful career in music. In fact, just a few months before he died, another Styne musical, *The Red Shoes*, opened on Broadway. Although short-lived, it was a testament to Styne's resilience and longevity. Born Julius Kerwin Styne in London, Styne's family emigrated to the United States and settled in Chicago in 1912. A child prodigy at the piano, Styne was performing with the Chicago, St. Louis and Detroit symphonies before the age of 10. In 1916, he published his first song "The Moth and the Flame" for teenage producer Mike Todd. As he got older, Styne became less interested in classical music, and more in composing popular songs. Hollywood soon took notice and Twentieth Century-Fox hired him for various musical chores. One of his first hits, with lyrics by Frank Loesser, was "I Don't Want to Walk Without You." In 1942, he formed a close collaboration with Sammy Cahn and wrote a string of Hit Parade hits and songs for movies (many for Frank Sinatra), including: "I've Heard That Song Before," "I'll Walk Alone," "Time After Time", "It's Been a Long, Long Time," "Let It Snow! Let It Snow! Let It Snow!" and the Oscar-winner, "Three Coins in the Fountain." From the late 1940s onward, Styne turned most of his talents to composing for the Broadway stage. His long-running shows include *High Button Shoes, Gentlemen Prefer Blondes, Peter Pan, Gypsy, Bells Are Ringing* and *Funny Girl.* A few of the hit songs from these shows are "Diamonds Are a Girl's Best Friend," "The Party's Over," "Just in Time," "Let Me Entertain You" and "People." Perhaps the most appropriate tribute to Styne was read into the Congressional Record in 1959 on the occasion of his 25th anniversary in show business: "The lives of Americans throughout our land as well as the lives of people throughout the corners of the world have been enriched by the artistry and genius of Jule Styne."

Great American
Songwriters

JAMES "JIMMY" VAN HEUSEN
1913-1990

Featured songs in this collection: "It Could Happen to You," "Moonlight Becomes You"

Born Edward Chester Babcock, in Syracuse, New York, Van Heusen is said to be a descendant of the grandfather of all American songwriters, Stephen Foster. What is certain is that he grew up next door to the Arluck family, which included composer Harold Arlen. Van Heusen took to the piano at an early age and was composing melodies by the time he entered high school in Syracuse. At age 16, he was an announcer on local radio station WSYR. In 1933, after attending Cazenovia Junior College, and studying piano at Syracuse University, Van Heusen accepted Arlen's invitation to come to New York and take over writing the score for the popular Cotton Club show in Harlem. The show Van Heusen worked on failed, but he had his first published song, "Harlem Hospitality." While trying to break into Tin Pan Alley, Van Heusen worked as a waiter and freight elevator operator. He wrote some of his songs on the elevator and plugged them to publishers during his off hours. Eventually, Van Heusen found work as a piano player at various firms, most importantly, Remicks. In 1938, while working there, he met bandleader Jimmy Dorsey and together they wrote Van Heusen's first hit, "It's the Dreamer in Me." At Remicks, Van Heusen also met Frank Sinatra and they developed a fast friendship. Bandleader Eddie De Lange and Van Heusen teamed up for several songs which culminated in the hit, "Darn That Dream," for the failed swing extravaganza *Swingin' the Dream.* In 1939, also at Remicks, Van Heusen met the man who would become his primary writing partner for the next two decades, lyricist Johnny Burke. Their string of hits included, "Polka Dots and Moonbeams," "Imagination" and the scores for most of the "Road" pictures starring Bing Crosby and Bob Hope. "Moonlight Becomes You" was the most notable hit to come from a "Road" picture. In the mid 1950s, after writing with several others, Van Heusen found a new partner in Sammy Cahn. In 1955, their score for the television version of *Our Town* won an Emmy Award. Also that year, their song "The Tender Trap" was an Oscar nominee and a big hit for Sinatra. Other Van Heusen hits with Sammy Cahn include, "My Kind of Town," "Where Love Has Gone" and "The Second Time Around." Other tunes Van Heusen wrote for movies include four Oscar-winners, "Swinging on a Star" (1944), "All the Way" (1957), "High Hopes" (1959) and "Call Me Irresponsible" (1963). With the exception of "Star," written with Burke, the other Oscar- winners were done with Cahn.

HARRY WARREN
1893-1981

Featured songs in this collection: "Innamorata," "That's Amore"

Like a short order cook, Harry Warren spent 30 years dishing up songs that were devoured by the American masses. Between 1935 and 1950, no one wrote more Top 10 hits. Not Irving Berlin, Cole Porter, or Richard Rodgers, and yet anonymity followed Warren persistently, like a shadow.
His musical legacy includes three Best Song Academy Awards: "Lullaby of Broadway," "You'll Never Know" and "Atchison, Topeka and the Santa Fe." Other standards for which he wrote the music include "42nd Street," "We're in the Money," "September in the Rain," "I Only Have Eyes for You," "The More I See You," "Chattanooga Choo Choo," "Jeepers Creepers" and "That's Amore." Most of his hits were written in collaboration with Al Dubin, Johnny Mercer and Mack Gordon. Born Salvatore Guaragna in Brooklyn, Warren was a self-taught pianist who began his career by plugging songs in Tin Pan Alley. With characteristic modesty, he discounted his natural gifts as a superb melodist during a 1980 interview in his Beverly Hills home. "I think you're just endowed that way, born with it," he said. "I think it's a God-given gift. That's the only excuse I can give you." If ever there was a "complete" composer, it was Warren. His compositions cut across musical idioms, displaying a versatility few of his contemporaries could match. It's too bad that the creator of some of America's most cherished song standards never enjoyed the popularity of his music.

KURT WEILL

1900-1950

Featured songs in this collection: "September Song," "Speak Low"

Whenever Bobby Darin or Louis Armstrong thunders through that ominous ode, "Mack the Knife," from *The Threepenny Opera,* they are paying tribute to its composer, Kurt Weill. The show, one of Weill's first major successes, was originally produced in Germany in 1928. The son of a cantor, Weill proved early on to be musically gifted. By the time he was 10, Weill was earning money as an accompanist in the orchestra of the Duke of Anhalt in his hometown of Dessau, Germany. In 1918, Weill entered the Berlin High School of Music. Though he studied the classics, to earn extra money Weill obligingly played piano in a Berlin beer garden. His first opera *The Protagonist* was written in 1924 to a surrealist text. The expressionistic score combined jazz and serious music and was successfully produced in Dresden. Weill made further use of jazz with his score for *The Czar Has Himself Photographed.* At about this time, he began writing the music for *Mahagonny,* a one-act play with a book by playwright, Bertolt Brecht, one of the century's greatest dramatists. He and Brecht then decided to update John Gay's *The Beggar's Opera* into *The Threepenny Opera.* The show was a smash and ran for almost five years in Germany alone after its opening. Brecht and Weill then expanded their earlier one-act sketch into a three-act opera, *The Rise and Fall of the City of Mahagonny,* a fantasy set in the American South. On opening night, Nazis started a riot during the play that the police had to quell. Weill then started work on a new play, *The Lake of Silver.* On February 19, 1933, the day after the show opened, the Reichstag burned and Weill and his wife, Lotte Lenya, fled Germany to Paris. After emigrating to America in 1935, Weill attempted to become an organic part of Broadway, because he thought this was the best place to build a tradition of American opera. Weill had several musical successes including *Knickerbocker Holiday* (1938), and, in 1941, *Lady in the Dark.* Two years later, Weill scored another hit with *One Touch of Venus,* which featured a book by S.J. Perelman and lyrics by famed wit, Ogden Nash. The show featured the hit song, "Speak Low," and starred Mary Martin. Weill's most ambitious show on Broadway was *Street Scene* (1947). In 1948, Weill collaborated with Alan Jay Lerner on *Love Life* which featured such songs as, "Green-Up Time," "Love Song," "Mr. Right" and "Here I'll Stay." In October 1949, *Lost in the Stars* premiered on Broadway. Based on Alan Paton's *Cry the Beloved Country,* it is a tale of of racial strife in South Africa. It had some of Weill's most haunting music, including the title song, and had a long run on Broadway. Before his untimely death he was working on a new musical based on *The Adventures of Huckleberry Finn.*

Great American
Songwriters

AREN'T YOU KIND OF GLAD WE DID?

Music and Lyrics by GEORGE GERSHWIN
and IRA GERSHWIN

BEWITCHED
from PAL JOEY

Words by LORENZ HART
Music by RICHARD RODGERS

Moderately, in 2

He's a fool and don't I know it. But a fool can have his charms.
Love's the same old sad sen - sa - tion. Late - ly I've not slept a wink

I'm in love and don't I show it, Like a babe in arms.
Since this half - pint im - i - ta - tion

Put me on the blink. I'm wild a - gain, Be - guiled a - gain, A

BABY, IT'S COLD OUTSIDE
from the Motion Picture NEPTUNE'S DAUGHTER

By FRANK LOESSER

BLUE SKIES
from BETSY

Words and Music by
IRVING BERLIN

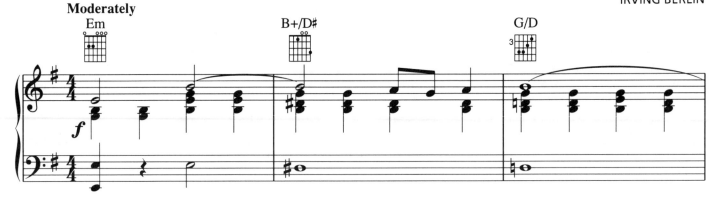

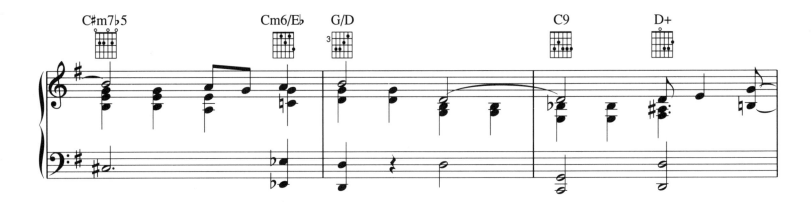

I was blue just as blue as I could
I should care if the wind blows east or

COME RAIN OR COME SHINE
from ST. LOUIS WOMAN

Words by JOHNNY MERCER
Music by HAROLD ARLEN

BY MYSELF
from BETWEEN THE DEVIL

Words by HOWARD DIETZ
Music by ARTHUR SCHWARTZ

CALL ME IRRESPONSIBLE

from the Paramount Picture PAPA'S DELICATE CONDITION

Words by SAMMY CAHN
Music by JAMES VAN HEUSEN

CHEEK TO CHEEK
from the RKO Radio Motion Picture TOP HAT

Words and Music by
IRVING BERLIN

CLOSE AS PAGES IN A BOOK

from UP IN CENTRAL PARK

Words by DOROTHY FIELDS
Music by SIGMUND ROMBERG

Expressively

DO I LOVE YOU BECAUSE YOU'RE BEAUTIFUL?

from CINDERELLA

Lyrics by OSCAR HAMMERSTEIN II
Music by RICHARD RODGERS

EV'RY TIME WE SAY GOODBYE
from SEVEN LIVELY ARTS

Words and Music by
COLE PORTER

8vb -

THE FOLKS WHO LIVE ON THE HILL

from HIGH, WIDE AND HANDSOME

Lyrics by OSCAR HAMMERSTEIN II
Music by JEROME KERN

Many men with lofty aims, Strive for lofty goals, Others play at smaller games, Being simpler souls. I am of the latter brand; All I want to do Is to find a spot of land

GEORGIA ON MY MIND

Words by STUART GORRELL
Music by HOAGY CARMICHAEL

GIGI

Words by ALAN JAY LERNER
Music by FREDERICK LOEWE

Slowly

Gi - gi, Am I a fool with-out a mind or have I mere-ly been too blind to re - a - lize? Oh

Gi - gi, Why you've been grow-ing up be - fore my eyes!

Gi - gi, You're not at all that fun - ny, awk - ward lit - tle girl I knew. Oh

GLAD TO BE UNHAPPY
from ON YOUR TOES

Words by LORENZ HART
Music by RICHARD RODGERS

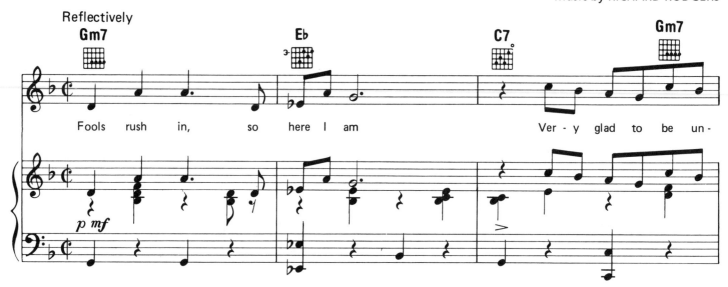

Fools rush in, so here I am Ver-y glad to be un-

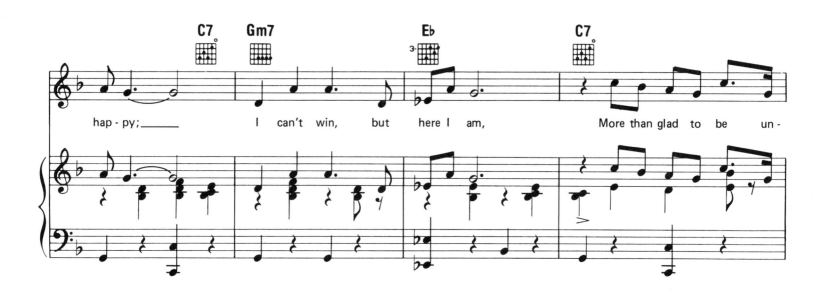

hap-py;_____ I can't win, but here I am, More than glad to be un-

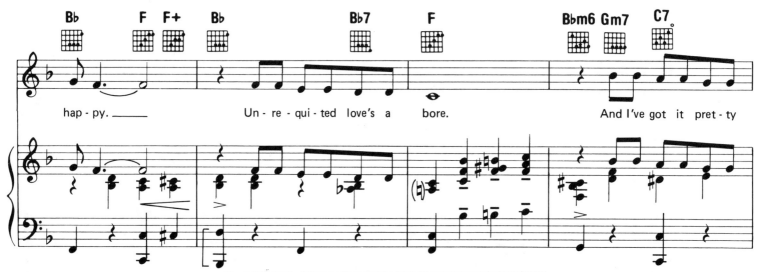

hap-py. _____ Un-re-qui-ted love's a bore. And I've got it pret-ty

HOW ARE THINGS IN GLOCCA MORRA

from FINIAN'S RAINBOW

Words by E.Y. HARBURG
Music by BURTON LANE

I CAN'T GET STARTED WITH YOU

from ZIEGFELD FOLLIES

Words by IRA GERSHWIN
Music by VERNON DUKE

I CAN'T GIVE YOU ANYTHING BUT LOVE

from BLACKBIRDS OF 1928

Words by DOROTHY FIELDS
Music by JIMMY McHUGH

I WISH I DIDN'T LOVE YOU SO

from the Paramount Picture THE PERILS OF PAULINE

Words and Music by
FRANK LOESSER

Slowly

Lyrics:
I wish I did-n't love you so, ___ My love for you, Should have fad-ed long a-go. ___ I wish I did-n't need your

I'LL BE SEEING YOU
from RIGHT THIS WAY

Lyric by IRVING KAHAL
Music by SAMMY FAIN

Ca - the - dral bells were toll - ing _____ And our hearts sang on, _____

_____ Was it the spell of Par - is _____ Or the A - pril dawn? _____

Who knows, _____ if we shall meet a - gain? _____

I'M OLD FASHIONED
from YOU WERE NEVER LOVELIER

Words by JOHNNY MERCER
Music by JEROME KERN

Moderately

I am not such a clev-er one A-bout the lat-est fads; I ad-mit I was nev-er one A-dored by lo-cal lads;

I'VE GOT YOU UNDER MY SKIN

from BORN TO DANCE

Words and Music by
COLE PORTER

IF EVER I WOULD LEAVE YOU
from CAMELOT

Words by ALAN JAY LERNER
Music by FREDERICK LOEWE

INNAMORATA
(Sweetheart)

from the Paramount Picture ARTISTS AND MODELS

Words by JACK BROOKS
Music by HARRY WARREN

Moderately slow and tenderly

If our lips should meet, in-nam-o-ra-ta, ___ kiss me, kiss me, sweet, in-nam-o-ra-ta. ___ Hold me close and

ISN'T IT ROMANTIC?

from the Paramount Picture LOVE ME TONIGHT

Words by LORENZ HART
Music by RICHARD RODGERS

IT COULD HAPPEN TO YOU

from the Paramount Picture AND THE ANGELS SING

Words by JOHNNY BURKE
Music by JAMES VAN HEUSEN

Lyrics: Do you be-lieve in charms and spells, in mys-tic words and mag-ic wands and wish-ing wells? Don't look so wise, don't

120

IT DON'T MEAN A THING
(If It Ain't Got That Swing)
from SOPHISTICATED LADIES

Words and Music by DUKE ELLINGTON
and IRVING MILLS

IT MIGHT AS WELL BE SPRING
from STATE FAIR

Lyrics by OSCAR HAMMERSTEIN II
Music by RICHARD RODGERS

Gracefully

I'm as rest-less as a wil-low in a wind-storm, I'm as
jump-y as a pup-pet on a string. I'd say that I had spring-
fe-ver, but I know it is-n't spring. I am

JUST IN TIME
from BELLS ARE RINGING

Words by BETTY COMDEN and ADOLPH GREEN
Music by JULE STYNE

no-where to go._____ Now you're here_____ and now I

know just where I'm go-ing, no more doubt or fear,_____ I've found my

way._____ For love came Just In Time._____ You found me

Just In Time_____ and changed my lone-ly life, that love-ly

day._____ day._____

LAST NIGHT
WHEN WE WERE YOUNG

Lyric by E.Y. HARBURG
Music by HAROLD ARLEN

LONG AGO
(And Far Away)
from COVER GIRL

Words by IRA GERSHWIN
Music by JEROME KERN

LOVE ME OR LEAVE ME

Lyrics by GUS KAHN
Music by WALTER DONALDSON

THE MAN THAT GOT AWAY

from the Motion Picture A STAR IS BORN

Lyric by IRA GERSHWIN
Music by HAROLD ARLEN

MOON RIVER

from the Paramount Picture BREAKFAST AT TIFFANY'S

Words by JOHNNY MERCER
Music by HENRY MANCINI

MY BUDDY

Lyrics by GUS KAHN
Music by WALTER DONALDSON

MOONLIGHT BECOMES YOU
from the Paramount Picture ROAD TO MOROCCO

Words by JOHNNY BURKE
Music by JAMES VAN HEUSEN

MY FUNNY VALENTINE
from BABES IN ARMS

Words by LORENZ HART
Music by RICHARD RODGERS

SATIN DOLL
from SOPHISTICATED LADIES

Words by JOHNNY MERCER and BILLY STRAYHORN
Music by DUKE ELLINGTON

PEOPLE
from FUNNY GIRL

Words by BOB MERRILL
Music by JULE STYNE

SEPTEMBER SONG
from the Musical Play KNICKERBOCKER HOLIDAY

Words by MAXWELL ANDERSON
Music by KURT WEILL

When I was a young man court-ing the girls, I played me a wait-ing
meet with the young men ear-ly in spring, They court you in song and

game; If a maid re-fused me with toss-ing curls, I
rhyme, They woo you with words and a clo-ver ring, But

let the old earth take a coup-le of whirls, While I plied her with tears in
if you ex-am-ine the goods they bring, They have lit-tle to of-fer but the

SMALL WORLD
from GYPSY

Words by STEPHEN SONDHEIM
Music by JULE STYNE

SOME ENCHANTED EVENING
from SOUTH PACIFIC

Lyrics by OSCAR HAMMERSTEIN II
Music by RICHARD RODGERS

SOPHISTICATED LADY

from SOPHISTICATED LADIES

Words and Music by DUKE ELLINGTON,
IRVING MILLS and MITCHELL PARISH

SOMEBODY LOVES ME

from SHE LOVES ME

Words by B.G. DeSYLVA and BALLARD MacDONALD
Music by GEORGE GERSHWIN
French Version by EMELIA RENAUD

THE SONG IS YOU
from MUSIC IN THE AIR

Lyrics by OSCAR HAMMERSTEIN II
Music by JEROME KERN

Lyrics:
I hear mu-sic when I look at you, _____ A beau-ti-ful theme of ev-'ry dream I ev-er knew, _____ Down deep in my heart, _____ I hear it play, _____ I feel it

SPEAK LOW
from the Musical Production ONE TOUCH OF VENUS

Words by OGDEN NASH
Music by KURT WEILL

STAR DUST

Words by MITCHELL PARISH
Music by HOAGY CARMICHAEL

...And now the pur-ple dusk of twi-light time steals a-cross the mead-ows of my heart. High up in the sky the lit-tle stars climb, al-ways re-mind-ing me that

STORMY WEATHER
(Keeps Rainin' All the Time)
from COTTON CLUB PARADE OF 1933

Lyric by TED KOEHLER
Music by HAROLD ARLEN

Slow lament

Don't know why _____ there's no sun up in the sky, Storm-y Weath-er, _____

Since my {man}{gal} and I _____ ain't to-geth-er, _____ keeps rain-in' all ___ the time. _____

Life is bare, _____ gloom and mis-'ry ev-'ry-where, Storm-y Weath-er, _____

Interlude

SWANEE

Words by IRVING CAESAR
Music by GEORGE GERSHWIN

THAT OLD BLACK MAGIC

from the Paramount Picture STAR SPANGLED RHYTHM

Words by JOHNNY MERCER
Music by HAROLD ARLEN

THAT'S AMORE
(That's Love)
from the Paramount Picture THE CADDY

Words by JACK BROOKS
Music by HARRY WARREN

Lyrics: In Na-po-li, where love is king, when boy meets girl, here's what they sing: When the moon hits your eye like a big piz-za pie, that's a-

THREE COINS IN THE FOUNTAIN

Words by SAMMY CAHN
Music by JULE STYNE

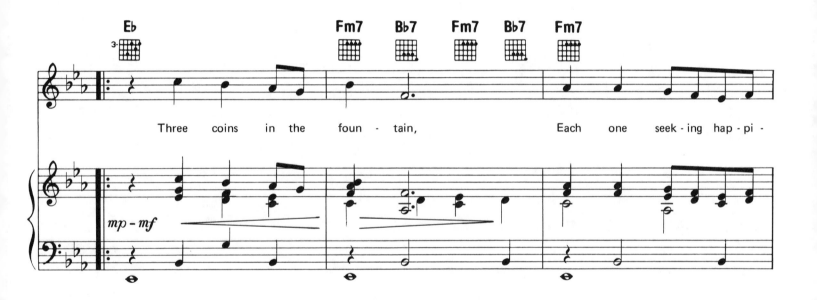

Three coins in the foun-tain, Each one seek-ing hap-pi-

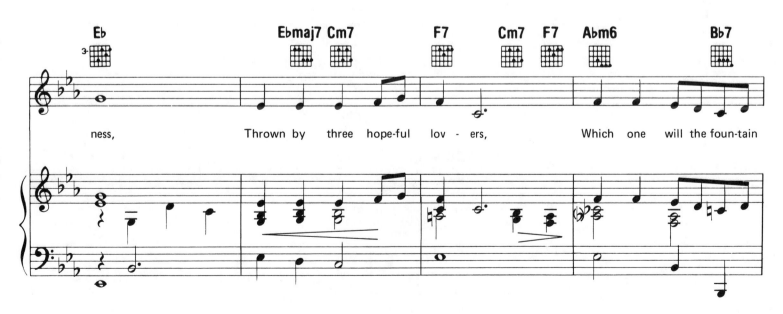

ness, Thrown by three hope-ful lov-ers, Which one will the foun-tain

THAT'S ENTERTAINMENT
from THE BAND WAGON

Words by HOWARD DIETZ
Music by ARTHUR SCHWARTZ

TOO DARN HOT
from KISS ME, KATE

Words and Music by
COLE PORTER

224

TOO LATE NOW

Words by ALAN JAY LERNER
Music by BURTON LANE

THE WAY YOU LOOK TONIGHT
from SWING TIME

Words by DOROTHY FIELDS
Music by JEROME KERN

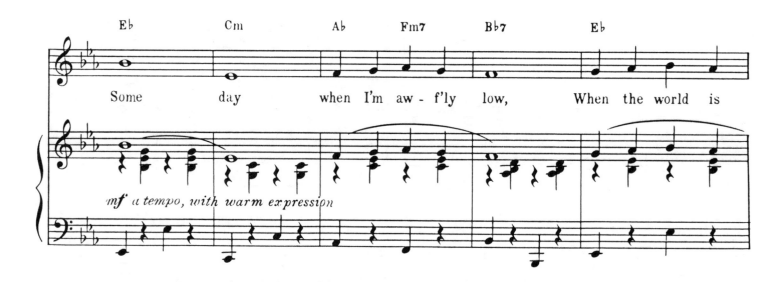

Some day when I'm aw-f'ly low, When the world is

cold, I will feel a glow just think-ing of you

WHAT'LL I DO?

from MUSIC BOX REVUE OF 1924

Words and Music by
IRVING BERLIN

YOU BROUGHT A NEW KIND OF LOVE TO ME

from the Paramount Picture THE BIG POND

Words and Music by SAMMY FAIN,
IRVING KAHAL and PIERRE NORMAN

Sweet one, _____ fair - er than the flow - ers, _____

YOU TOOK ADVANTAGE OF ME
from PRESENT ARMS

Words by LORENZ HART
Music by RICHARD RODGERS

Classic Collections Of Your Favorite Songs

arranged for piano, voice, and guitar.

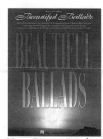

Beautiful Ballads

A massive collection of 87 songs, including: April In Paris • Autumn In New York • Call Me Irresponsible • Cry Me A River • I Wish You Love • I'll Be Seeing You • If • Imagine • Isn't It Romantic? • It's Impossible (Somos Novios) • Mona Lisa • Moon River • People • The Way We Were • A Whole New World (Aladdin's Theme) • and more.

00311679 ....$17.95

Irving Berlin Anthology

A comprehensive collection of 61 timeless songs with a bio, song background notes, and photos. Songs include: Always • Blue Skies • Cheek To Cheek • God Bless America • Marie • Puttin' On The Ritz • Steppin' Out With My Baby • There's No Business Like Show Business • White Christmas • (I Wonder Why?) You're Just In Love • and more.

00312493 ....$19.95

The Best Standards Ever Volume 1 (A-L)

72 beautiful ballads, including: All The Things You Are • Bewitched • Can't Help Lovin' Dat Man • Don't Get Around Much Anymore • Getting To Know You • God Bless' The Child • Hello, Young Lovers • I Got It Bad And That Ain't Good • It's Only A Paper Moon • I've Got You Under My Skin • The Lady Is A Tramp • Little White Lies.

00359231 ....$15.95

The Best Standards Ever Volume 2 (M-Z)

72 songs, including: Makin' Whoopee • Misty • Moonlight In Vermont • My Funny Valentine • Old Devil Moon • The Party's Over • People Will Say We're In Love • Smoke Gets In Your Eyes • Strangers In The Night • Tuxedo Junction • Yesterday.

00359232 ....$15.95

The Big Book of Standards

86 classics essential to any music library, including: April In Paris • Autumn In New York • Blue Skies • Cheek To Cheek • Heart And Soul • I Left My Heart In San Francisco • In The Mood • Isn't It Romantic? • Mona Lisa • Moon River • The Nearness Of You • Out Of Nowhere • Spanish Eyes • Star Dust • Stella By Starlight • That Old Black Magic • They Say It's Wonderful • What Now My Love • and more.

00311667 ....$19.95

Classic Jazz Standards

56 jazz essentials: All the Things You Are • Don't Get Around Much Anymore • How Deep Is the Ocean • In the Wee Small Hours of the Morning • Polka Dots and Moonbeams • Satin Doll • Skylark • Tangerine • Tenderly • What's New? • and more.

00310310 ....$16.95

I'll Be Seeing You: 50 Songs of World War II

A salute to the music and memories of WWII, including a year-by-year chronology of events on the homefront, dozens of photos, and 50 radio favorites of the GIs and their families back home, including: Boogie Woogie Bugle Boy • Don't Sit Under The Apple Tree (With Anyone Else But Me) • I Don't Want To Walk Without You • I'll Be Seeing You • Moonlight In Vermont • There's A Star-Spangled Banner Waving Somewhere • You'd Be So Nice To Come Home To • and more.

00311698 ....$19.95

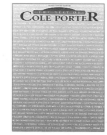

Best of Cole Porter

38 of his classics, including: All Of You • Anything Goes • Be A Clown • Don't Fence Me In • I Get A Kick Out Of You • In The Still Of The Night • Let's Do It (Let's Fall In Love) • Night And Day • You Do Something To Me • and many

00311577 ....$14.95

Remember This One?

43 classics, including: Ac-cent-tchu-ate The Positive • Ain't She Sweet • Autumn Leaves • (The Original) Boogie Woogie • A Good Man Is Hard To Find • I Wanna Be Loved By You • Mister Sandman • Sentimental Journey • Sioux City Sue • Unchained Melody • and more.

00384600 ....$12.95

The Best of Rodgers & Hammerstein

A capsule of 26 classics from this legendary duo. Songs include: Climb Ev'ry Mountain • Edelweiss • Getting To Know You • I'm Gonna Wash That Man Right Outa My Hair • My Favorite Things • Oklahoma • The Surrey With The Fringe On Top • You'll Never Walk Alone • and more.

00308210 ....$12.95

The Best Songs Ever

80 must-own classics, including: All I Ask Of You • Body And Soul • Crazy • Endless Love • Fly Me To The Moon • Here's That Rainy Day • In The Mood • Love Me Tender • Memory • Moonlight In Vermont • My Funny Valentine • People • Satin Doll • Save The Best For Last • Somewhere Out There • Strangers In The Night • Tears In Heaven • A Time For Us • The Way We Were • When I Fall In Love • You Needed Me • and more.

00359224 ....$19.95

Torch Songs

Sing your heart out with this collection of 59 sultry jazz and big band melancholy masterpieces, including: Angel Eyes • Cry Me A River • I Can't Get Started • I Got It Bad And That Ain't Good • I'm Glad There Is You • Lover Man (Oh, Where Can You Be?) • Misty • My Funny Valentine • Stormy Weather • and many more! 224 pages.

00490446 ....$16.95

FOR MORE INFORMATION, SEE YOUR LOCAL MUSIC DEALER,
OR WRITE TO:

HAL•LEONARD
CORPORATION

7777 W. BLUEMOUND RD. P.O. BOX 13819 MILWAUKEE, WI 53213